# Moving to Belize - Not for Me!

G. Roebuck

Cover Photo: Graeme Douglas

ISBN-13: 978-1500395032

ISBN-10: 150039503X

ii

*He began to build a condo, but the labor cost was high,*

*His partner stole his money, which left him high and dry,*

*His land is still a mudhole, where you sink up to your knees*

*And he's just another gringo in Belize.*

—Lyrics to Jerry Jeff Walker's *Gringo in Belize.*

# CONTENTS

# Moving to Belize - Not for Me!

Moving to Belize – Not for Me!

## Introduction

The chance to retire to a warm sunny Caribbean destination where the English language is not a problem and the cost of living is easily affordable on a basic pension may sound too good to be true. On the surface, the Central American country of Belize has so many things going for it. This former British commonwealth country is sparsely inhabited with a population of less than 360,000 inhabitants. It has the second largest reef in the world after the Great Barrier Reef, and 60% of the country is rainforest. Rich in exotic birds and wildlife, this country should be every naturalist's perfect paradise.

Photo: Dennis Jarvis

Soft white sandy beaches lapped by warm Caribbean waters make snorkeling, swimming and diving a delight, while sport fishing can be an exciting pastime. Broad rivers irrigate this 200-mile long country, keeping it lush and green.

Historically, Belize was inhabited by the Mayans who have left an incredible legacy of ruined remains from their native culture. Who knows what treasures still remain undiscovered in the dense and unchartered jungle of this developing country?

With an ease of permanent residency which provides few difficulties for most potential expats from a westernized country, Belize really should be as popular with immigrants as the Yukon during the Klondike Gold Rush.

Belize is frequently listed by International Living and other sources as one of the best places in the world for retirees, second only to its near neighbor, Panama. It ticks all the boxes as being a stable, peaceful country with a wonderful tropical climate and low cost of living. Add the stunning natural beauty, amazing wildlife and natural resources, including oil, and it sounds like it is truly "Paradise Found".

That's certainly what I was led to believe as I began my research looking for a place to retire in the sun. More particularly, I was seeking a safe tax-free haven that would protect my hard-earned assets, keeping them fully available in order for me to enjoy early retirement with a sensible, but not necessarily decadent, standard of living.

However, lack of reliable services, concerns about personal and property safety, lack of any recycling or eco-friendly awareness, filthy gutters, dumping of garbage, lack of availability of certain foods, expensive utilities, few sandy beaches outside the cayes and a host of other unexpected problems caused me to reconsider whether Moving to Belize was really the best thing for me.

For others similarly seeking an affordable place to live in the sun, here is my experience of living in Belize and why ultimately it was not the place for me to settle permanently. This book outlines the benefits of Belize as a tax haven, but also lists the unexpected problems that living in Belize can create.

For anyone looking for a well-balanced account of life in Belize – the pluses and the minuses – from someone who has no motive for "selling" you a dream, this book is a valuable resource. Hopefully it will help you make an informed decision about whether moving to Belize is right for you, based on the factual personal account of someone who has already traveled the same road. Although Belize may be the perfect solution for some, ultimately I found that Moving to Belize was definitely Not for Me. Here's why…

## Belize as a Retirement Haven

Having been drawn by the Belizean Retirement Program (QRP), I began my quest for information about retiring to Belize in earnest. I spent a small fortune on ebooks giving me the insider guide to other trailblazers who had already moved to Belize. Next step was a visit to this Central American country to research the best place to live and checkout the culture and lifestyle that my wife and I were about to permanently embrace.

Our planned visit was extremely useful and fruitful, but not at all in the way I had expected. I found some things that surprised me positively, but there were other discoveries which I found extremely difficult to imagine myself being reconciled with. After all my hopes, plans and research, I eventually had to cross Belize off my shortlist of places to retire, despite the financial positives that this tax-free haven would have afforded me.

Here is the book I wish had been available to me when I was doing my research! I hope that this honest account of my experience in planning to retire permanently to Belize, and my reasons for not doing so, will help others to make up their mind whether Belize is the perfect place for them or not.

I accept that not everyone is looking for the same nirvana that I was, and I have met some American, Canadian and British expats who have happily made the move to Belize without regrets. However, sadly I have met others who took everything they read and were told about Belize at face value, and lived to regret not doing their own background research more carefully.

Photo: Jim Mitchum

For those considering moving to Belize I would earnestly suggest:

- Do your own research rather than trusting the spiel of realtors, expat guides, vacation companies or those offering expensive conferences, who clearly have a vested interest in your moving to Belize
- Read balanced accounts of life in Belize through blogs, forums, books and websites written by expats. Be wary of trusting glossy tourism or real estate brochures that may be selective about the facts they give you about the lifestyle in Belize

- Talk, use forums and chat online with people who have already made the move to Belize and ask them direct questions about their lifestyle choices
- Draw up a checklist of what you really need your retirement destination to have, and don't compromise on your non-negotiable points
- Don't be blinded by just one or two outstanding positives. In my case this was incredibly difficult as I thought the financial benefits would far outweigh all the niggling negatives. In the end, they did not.
- Visit Belize at least once, ideally for a stay of two months or longer. Live as a local in a rented house in your chosen location before making any long-term or irreversible decisions

There are no shortcuts to doing due diligence. Making a permanent move to a new country is a huge decision which should not be done in haste. No research is ever wasted. I hope you discover that Belize is exactly what you expect and are looking for, allowing you to break out from your old life and start afresh in an exciting and challenging environment. But in my case, after all my deliberations I found that it was definitely a case of Moving to Belize - Not for Me!

## Facts About Belize

Belize is a small English-speaking country in Central America next to Mexico and Guatemala. Bordering the Caribbean Sea, it benefits from a tropical climate and an easy laid-back lifestyle. Known for its tax advantages and banking, the country's main source of income is from tourism. The extensive Belize Reef is the second largest reef system in the world and, together with the famous Blue Hole, it offers spectacular snorkeling and diving.

Belize is a peaceful country with a population of around 328,000 inhabitants. The capital city is Belmopan, although the port of Belize City and the island of Ambergris Caye are generally better known. The country has a colonial past and only received its independence from the UK in 1981. Its currency is the Belizean dollar, which is currently pegged at 2:1 to the US dollar.

The country's main exports are fish and marine products, sugar, bananas, citrus, molasses, wood and crude oil. The country has weak economic growth and a large public debt so general infrastructure and services are poor. According to the 2010 Poverty Assessment, four out of 10 people in Belize live in poverty.

Belize is one of the most popular places for those looking for an affordable lifestyle, particularly after retirement. The ease of acquiring permanent residency, tax breaks, climate, ability for foreigners to own property and being an English speaking country using English law are all plus points for those looking for a place to retire in the sun.

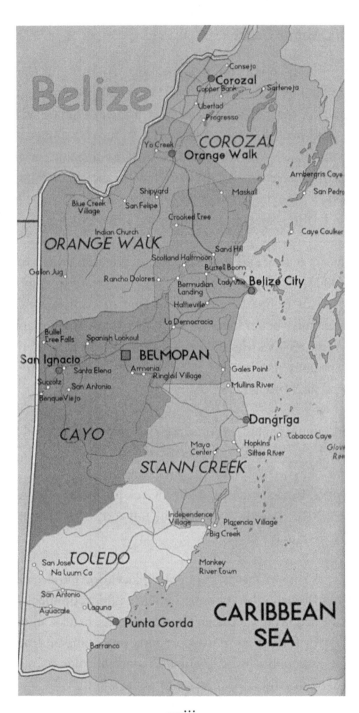

## 1. Choosing Where to Live in Belize

Belize is divided into six districts, plus Ambergris Caye:
- Corozal
  Orange Walk
- Belize district including Belize City
- Cayo district around San Ignacio
- Stann Creek
- Toledo
- Ambergris Caye

**Corozal**

The Corozal district is in the far north of Belize. This area is particularly popular with expats as it is just a short boat or bus ride from Mexico for shopping and medical facilities.

Corozal Town is just 9 miles south of the Mexican border and has a number of hotels and restaurants. Corozal was built on the ancient Mayan city of Santa Rita and there are a number of excavations. Smaller local villages include Sarteneja and the Mennonite village of Little Belize.

The Corozal shoreline borders sheltered Corozal Bay, also known by its Mexican name of Chetumal Bay. Unfortunately there are no sandy beaches for hanging your hammock as the area is thick with mangroves. The one exception is at Corozal Bay Resort which was enterprising enough to import tons of sand and create its own manmade beach. Regrettably, the waters here are murky due to river deposits and sea grass beds so it is far from being a

Caribbean dream destination. There is also no diving in this area without taking a boat trip out to the reef.

Two trips of interest from Corozal Town are the 15 minute boat ride to the Cerros ruins, a 400BC Maya trading center, and the longer boat ride up the New River to Lamanai. This was an important ceremonial center for the Maya and the 26-mile journey offers the chance to encounter turtles, crocodiles, iguanas and other wildlife along the way.

## Orange Walk

North of Cayo, Orange Walk is a small but interesting district bordering Mexico and Guatemala. It is inhabited mainly by Mennonite settlers and Spanish-speaking descendants of the Maya and Mestizo people.

Nicknamed "Sugar City", parts of the original forest savannah are covered in sugar cane supplying a sugar refinery at Honey Camp Lagoon. Fortunately, 280,000 acres of tropical rainforest is protected as a reserve under the Rio Bravo Conservation Project. La Milpa and Lamanai are the sites of well-preserved Mayan ruins and the best way to access Lamanai is by boat.

Orange Walk Town is only 90 minutes by bus from Belize City. Buses leave and return on the hour for those in

## Belize district

My first exploratory visit to Belize involved arriving by cruise ship into the port of Belize City. The contrast between shipboard life and local life in this shanty town could not have been more marked. I had chosen to stay in a local hotel which I expected to be to a three-star standard, but it clearly was not.

An even greater culture shock awaited me. The main street near the port was unpaved and had raw sewage running down open channels on either side of the road. This had to be crossed to get into any of the local shops, and I use the term "shop" loosely. These basic buildings had very little stock inside, whether I visited the chemist or the grocery store. Provisions were stacked on the dusty floor and there was very little available even in the most common healthcare items such as antiseptics, painkillers and plasters.

Around the port there was a flurry of activity with enterprising locals offering their services as guides, but elsewhere there was little sign of any useful activity.

We were warned ahead of time that opportunistic theft was rife which added to the feeling of wariness and mistrust we had on arriving in this shockingly third world city. It was not a good start and certainly not what I had expected.

As well as suffering a high crime rate, Belize City has little to offer visitors wanting a beach vacation. Most of the coast is lined with a retaining wall to prevent erosion. If you do manage to get into the water, it is thick with sea grass. The water is unpleasantly murky due to the proximity to the port and the rivers that deposit mud, dirt and more in the estuary.

## Cayo district

Visitors considering moving to Belize will either love or hate the Cayo district. Despite being the largest district in Belize, it has limited infrastructure and services that we might take for granted elsewhere. The Cayo district is in the mountains in the west of the country and it includes the Belizean capital, Belmopan. The two main towns are San Ignacio (the regional capital) and Santa Elena. The cost of renting a simple home here with indoor plumbing and electricity would be around US$300-400 per month.

There are several rural villages in Cayo and the area is rich in pre-Columbian Mayan sites including Caracol, Xunantunich, El Pilar and Cahal Peck. It is very cheap to build a home and live there, but that is because there is very little demand. This was not my idea of comfortable retirement, but for some, the lack of consumerism is exactly what they are looking for. It is the perfect place for those dreaming of trading the rat race for a simpler, more peaceful existence.

The Cayo district is ideal for those wanting to live a self-sufficient life, perhaps growing oranges and bananas. It is not the place for those who rely on 21$^{st}$ century communications. If this sounds like your kind of paradise, then you should definitely check out this scenic area of jungle, mighty rivers and serene pastures of grazing cattle and horses.

This agricultural area is home to communities of Mennonites who still drive their horse-drawn carts, raise livestock and live a simple life devoted to their religious beliefs, exactly as they did in the 19<sup>th</sup> century.

## Stann Creek

The best thing about Stann Creek is that it has some wonderful sandy beaches making it a good choice for those wanting a beach lifestyle. There are plenty of hotels and resorts with bars and restaurants and the reef is a short boat trip away for snorkelers and divers. While the mainland is lined with mangroves, much of the Stann Creek area is made up of a series of beautiful offshore sandy cayes.

Belize's most popular beach is at Placencia, a 16-mile long peninsula with beaches made up of coarse brown sand along the eastern side. The sand can get very hot underfoot compared to the white sands of the cayes. However, the area is excellent for fishing, sailing, snorkeling and kayaking.

## Toledo district

The Toledo district is the most southern of the six districts. Although it is the least visited area for tourists, it is also the most colorful when it comes to wildlife and scenic natural beauty. Toledo has huge areas of pristine rainforest jungle, extensive cave systems, coastal lowlands and a scattering of offshore cayes.

Living in this 1,795 square–mile (4,649 sq.km) district is the highest concentration of indigenous peoples including the Garifuna, Mestizo, Creole and East Indians. You will also find a large community of German-speaking

Mennonites and an expat population that originated when US Confederates arrived looking for refuge at the end of the American Civil War around 1865.

This emerging destination is slowly being brought into the 20$^{th}$ century, if not the 21$^{st}$, with the completion of the paved Southern Highway allowing a more regular bus service. Those interested in seeing more of this area will find it is a mainly agricultural district producing corn, coffee, cacao beans, rice and citrus. Coastal communities provide a small-scale fishing industry diving for conch, lobster and other shellfish from their dugout canoes.

Whether the increasing tourism will make or mar this area remains to be seen. The protected wildness areas, waterfalls, abundant birds, wildlife and excellent snorkeling, kayaking and swimming off the Sapodilla Cayes are attracting the attention of international eco-tourists. The wealth of Mayan ruins in Toledo enhances its attraction with a royal palace and ceremonial centers at Nim Li Punit (Big Hat) and Uxbenka (Old Place).

**Ambergris Caye**

Ambergris Caye is totally different from other parts of Belize and is the most popular area of Belize for tourists and retirees. Currently it attracts 40% of all visitors to Belize. This beautiful 25-mile long island is developing fast, although condos and hotels are mercifully restricted to three storys in height; no higher than a coco palm tree.

This American-influenced community with its laid-back Caribbean lifestyle has fewer locals and more ex-pats, which makes it more expensive and generally more civilized than other parts of Belize. However there are few cars as locals rely mainly on golf carts to get around and transport goods. This maintains the island's unhurried pace of life and informal atmosphere

Ambergris Caye has white sandy beaches, a huge mangrove swamp and excellent snorkeling and diving on the stunning Belize Barrier Reef. Some resorts clear away the coastal sea grass and garbage which can spoil the beaches elsewhere on the caye.

Ambergris Caye is quite the opposite of Belize City and is not typical Belize. Some visitors describe San Pedro as "Little America". Although pretty much everything is available in terms of home comforts for the ex-pat, it is expensive.

Some people love the laid back lifestyle, hanging out on the beach drinking rum punches, while others abhor it. All this transplanted American lifestyle comes at a financial cost. Expensive by Belizean standards, life on Ambergris is about the same price as any other Caribbean destination. It is an exciting place to live, but it is not the place to choose to settle for those on a tight financial budget as you must be able to embrace the higher cost of the island lifestyle.

The cayes lying to the south of Ambergris, such as Caye Caulker, are as yet unexploited and remain popular with backpackers and divers. However, the beaches are small and do not have pristine white sands. Like much of the Belize coastline, Caye Caulker is lined with mangroves so you need to head to the east of the island if you are looking for a sandy beach. Beware of swimming in the channel known as "the split" on this caye. Currents can be strong and there are no lifeguards if you find yourself in difficulty.

While a holiday home in the rainforest or on a quiet beach may be an idyllic dream, it may not be practical for those looking to retire, work or live permanently in the area. The best way to see if this is the life for you is to rent somewhere initially and see what does and doesn't work for you. It's common sense really, but you would be surprised at how many people follow their "gut instinct", act on impulse and live to regret it. Being open-minded is key to finding the right place for you and your family to settle and be happy.

## 2. Buying a House in Belize

There are no restrictions on foreigners owning land and real estate in Belize, excluding nationally protected land. Once you have found your dream home, you should make a formal offer to the seller, preferably through a local realtor. You will be required to make a deposit of 10% pending the legal negotiations which usually take 2-3 months to complete.

Belize has all types of housing in some beautiful natural locations, whether you want beach, island or rainforest living. Like anywhere else in the world, not all beautiful places have a beautiful lifestyle. For those who want the security and familiarity of a more metropolitan lifestyle, there are many expat communities where homes and apartments are already built and are part of a community with a pool and social life built-in.

If you are searching for a remote, unspoiled location where you can live happily with your own company, and that of the resident local wildlife, there are plenty of places on the mainland and on the cayes where you can buy land and build your own home. However, there are few building regulations and experienced builders available. If you are not equipped to do much of the building work yourself, or at least closely supervise and instruct worker as you go, you are unlikely to get a satisfactory home to live in.

Kitchen units, floor and walls tiles, white goods and bathroom fitments may need to be imported to achieve the standard you are used to.

Water and electricity connections are available in many towns but maintaining the infrastructure with limited manpower and resources can be a challenge. Power and service outages should be expected from time to time. Sewer systems and waste management are improving but are not generally up to western standards. At the time I was in Belize, there were no recycling services. Glass soda and beer bottles may have a returnable fee so you get a few cents back, but more importantly the used bottles can be sterilized and reused to be more eco-friendly to the environment.

Most utility services are provided by a monopoly in Belize which does not bode well for either standards of service or costs. The government Public Utilities Commission was set up to ensure fair prices, but what you may take for granted in other parts of the world may not necessarily happen in Belize.

Many rural areas lack any sort of infrastructure so you may have to generate your own electricity and pump your own water, which must be filtered before being considered safe to drink. There is often no proper sanitation in rural areas which can lead to disease and poor health, particularly for local children who may also be suffering from malnutrition and poverty. Those considering moving to Belize need to face up to whether they can cope with living in a country where they may be presented with such heart-rending issues on a regular basis.

## 3. Cost of Buying a Home in Belize

Most people choose to rent when they move to Belize, at least initially. You can rent a house from little as US$300 a month up to $850, depending upon where you want to be located.

It is possible for foreigners to buy real estate, land or property in Belize for much less than other Caribbean destinations. For example, condos on Ambergris Caye can be bought for as little as US$125,000 and up, but an additional 10% stamp duty will also be levied as part of the closing costs.

It is best to check with a local realtor to find out what you can realistically expect for your budget in your chosen area. Realtors are also the best people to advise you on what additional costs you need to budget into your purchase costs.

## 4. Getting Connected to Utilities

### Electricity

Although Belize is advertised as a great place to live on a fixed income, it is not the cheapest place to live when it comes to utilities. Prices for services such as electricity and sewage are controlled by the government Public Utilities Commission but they are still much higher than in the USA.

Electricity in Belize is 110 volts, the same as in the USA. However, it is about twice as expensive, so air conditioning and electrical home appliances are considered a real luxury. There are also frequent outages and power surges which can quickly take their toll on complicated circuit boards in modern-day dishwashers, washing machines and similar electrical items.

The initial connection fee for a domestic electricity supply is around US$100 and a refundable deposit may also be required. Electricity costs around US$0.25 per kWh for residential use in Belize compared to $0.01796 in the USA (Florida 2013 prices after first 500 kWh charged at $0.076). For this reason many people opt to stay off the grid and use solar panels or a diesel/gasoline generator to provide power, especially in more remote areas.

For cooking, laundry, refrigeration and water heating, butane gas cylinders are more reliable and economical than electricity. A 100-pound tank of butane costs around US$60 and lasts about a month for an average household.

Some residents make use of Belize's endless sunshine and install solar panels to supply them with electricity for essentials such as refrigeration and lights. These are available from a couple in Cayo who moved to Belize several years ago and saw the need for solar technology.

Getting connected to local services may be vital for you when you first move to Belize, but it can take weeks. On the other hand, some people find themselves connected within a day! Anger and an impatient attitude generally get you nowhere; in fact it often results in an even slower rate of progress. Persistence in following up your application daily in a courteous, polite manner at least prevents your application from being totally ignored. Bear in mind that many of the utilities and commodities in Belize are run as monopolies. Be prepared to deal with companies that are inefficient and corrupt, although successive governments do appear to be addressing these issues.

**Water**

Piped water and sewage services are available in most towns but many homes still rely on local wells for water. Expats are advised to drink bottled water for safety. Westerners do not have the same resistance to waterborne disease and bacteria which may be present in local tap water. I consider the small cost of bottled water well worth paying to avoid any possibility of a stomach upset or more serious diseases such as typhoid or hepatitis A.

## 5. Availability of Communications

### Cable TV

Cable TV is very affordable in Belize with around 100 channels available starting at a monthly fee of US$25. Most channels are in English and include some popular North American channels such as CBS and NBC.

### Cell Phones

Cell phone technology is a little behind that of the USA, and prices are much higher. The local "Digicell" service offers packages of 200 minutes per month for around US$50, which works out at around US$0.25 per minute. Prepaid cell phone services cost even more per minute.

If you bring an overseas cell phone with you, you may need to have it unlocked (US$25 at the international airport shops) and then install a new SIM card. Calls using a prepaid phone card are around US$0.25 per minute, the same as using a public payphone, or you can arrange a monthly phone plan starting at US$25. International calls are more expensive and, depending upon your payment plan, can be up to US$1 per minute.

### Telephone Land Lines

Getting utilities connected is generally the first challenge for new arrivals in Belize. I found the telephone company, Belize Telemedia Ltd was the worst of a bad lot. I later discovered that the company has a virtual monopoly on telephone services. Consequently customer service was not high on their agenda and repairs, connections and improvements were unbelievably slow. Complaints seem to fall on deaf ears and when you do manage to engage with a representative of the company their couldn't-care-less attitude and arrogance were something I found hard to accept from a national company.

Telephone land lines are more reasonable than cell phones with monthly charges including line rental ranging from US$30-80, depending upon the level of service you require. Installation costs about $60 with an additional deposit of around $100. However, most people simply opt for a cellphone and/or a Voice Over Internet Provider (VOIP) service.

## Internet

The Internet is available everywhere except in the most remote areas of Belize. There may be a cost for installation, connection and modem rental. Budget at least US$50 per month for basic internet services and more for high-speed and DSL connections.

If you have internet access, it can be wise to open a Skype or BTL Webtalk account for VOIP services to chat with family and friends back home. There are circulating reports that BTL interferes with internet services such as Skype and Vonage, and users in some locations are forced to use the BTL internet service called Webtalk.

Monthly costs are covered in more detail in Chapter 10-General Cost of Living in Belize

## 6. Mail

The Belize postal service never ceased to impress me whenever I had to rely on their services. Mail boxes were emptied each workday morning at 10 a.m. and local delivery in the towns was 1-3 days. International mail delivery was less predictable, taking anything from 5 days to several weeks, even to the USA. However, there are few places in the world where you can still mail a postcard overseas for less than US$0.25.

Most communities have mail boxes available for rent, although if you opt to live in a town and clearly display your name/and or address, in theory you can have mail delivered to your door. The problem here is that few residential buildings actually have an official address. Parcels are always held at the post office for collection. If you receive a parcel from overseas, expect to pay duty, insurance and any freight surcharges.

If you come and go from Belize, the Belize Postal Service operates mail forwarding and mail holding services.

DHL and FedEx both have offices in Belize City and they offer the usual pricey but guaranteed services worldwide.

One tip I did learn was to always add the words "Central America" to your address for international mail. Many mail sorting services think that Belize is in Africa and your mail can go on a long and circuitous route quite unnecessarily. Do not abbreviate "Central America" to "C.A." or it may be mistaken for California. Just one of the joys of living off the main drag!

## 7. Staying in Touch

Staying in touch with family and friends back home can be very important to make it easier to settle in any new country. Belize is very easy to reach with regular affordable flights from the USA. It is just a 2½ hour flight from Dallas, making it quicker to reach Belize than Washington D.C.!

With few travel restrictions for Belize residents (check the visa section of Moving to Belize – Not for Me for exceptions to the rule), it is possible to make regular visits back home if you wish to do so.

Families and friends may be happy to visit if you choose to live on the beach or in some of the more developed areas such as Ambergris Caye and in the Corocal area. However, if you opt for mountain living, a small local house in the jungle may be more challenging for having family to visit. This may be an important issue when you decide where you want to put down permanent roots.

## 8. Furniture and Appliances

Anyone making the move to Belize should take advantage of the ability to import furniture, a vehicle and personal belongings as part of the QRP residency visa program. Wooden furniture made by the Mennonites in Belize is beautifully crafted but it can be rather uncomfortable if you are used to recliner sofas and overstuffed armchairs.

Handcrafted wooden tables, bed frames and chest of drawers can easily be sourced when you arrive, but you may want to import other items which are impossible to find in Belize. Good quality footwear, kitchen appliances, electronics, mattresses, books, specialist tools and sports equipment are well worth paying the necessary shipping and import costs to make your new life in Belize more comfortable.

Shipping by sea is far less expensive than by air, but it can take weeks, Make sure all the necessary paperwork is in place to avoid even further delays and additional costs. Customs duty is calculated upon the value of the goods in your home country, plus insurance, freight and sales tax. It generally works out at between 20-50% of the value of the items.

This duty is waived for those who are granted permanent residency, but conditions apply, so do check the current details on the Belize government website. For example, those who qualify for the QRP residency program for retirees are allowed to import their used household items duty-free within the first year of receiving their visa.

## 9. Managing Local Staff

Expats moving to Belize often hire staff to cook, clean and take care of their children. The minimum wage for domestic staff is currently US$1.50 per hour (BZ$3) although it is higher if you can find someone with experience.

Skilled nannies can command a wage of US$60 to US$150 per week, and higher if there is more than one child in their care. Nannies rarely live-in and are employed for an agreed 6-8 hours per day with paid overtime for longer hours.

## 10. General Cost of Living in Belize

One major reason why many people consider moving to Belize is the belief that their pension or fixed income will go much further in a developing country. Although this is true of some items, such as buying a home and eating out, the overall cost of living in Belize can be surprisingly high.

Photo: Isaac Peterson

Like many developing countries, the cost of living in Belize is lower if you live like a local. However for most expats who have become accustomed to certain standards when it comes to food choices, standards of housing, availability of utilities and social life, adjustment can be difficult.

Approximate monthly costs in US$ should typically be budgeted as follows:

Rent Small House or Condo   $700-$1200

| | |
|---|---|
| Electricity | $200-270 (with careful use!) |
| Butane | $60 |
| Water | $25 |
| Cable TV | $25+ |
| Telephone land line | $30-80 |
| Cell phone | $25-100 |
| Internet | $50+ |
| Groceries | $300 |
| Entertainment | $200 |
| Miscellaneous | $200 |
| Total | $1785- 2570 per month |

More detailed costs for connection and a breakdown of services are covered in chapters 4 and 5.

## 11. Groceries

Most immigrants are prepared to make compromises, but there are certain things that they are likely to crave from their home country. Many of these items are available in Belize, but at a hugely inflated price. Demand is low and the cost of sourcing and importing small quantities of any item naturally raises the price considerably.

If you picture yourself getting groceries in Belize it will certainly not involve facing heavy traffic on a four-lane highway, searching for a parking space and pushing a shopping cart up and down the well-lit aisles of a giant superstore, picking from an endless choice of products. In Belize you are more likely to find yourself strolling down a local dirt road and visiting various vendors specializing in fish or fresh produce that is freshly picked or caught that morning. For some, that is a definite plus; for others it is a novelty that quickly wears off. Convenience food and a choice of familiar brands are not luxuries you will find in Belize, even in larger towns such as Belize City. There is no Sams Club or Costco, no prepared salads and no specialist bakery or low-fat items.

Fresh fruit and vegetables can be found on open stalls and markets and are similar to those found anywhere else in the world. Bananas, mangoes, oranges, papayas, watermelon, pineapples, lettuce, cauliflower, cabbage, zucchini, tomatoes and peppers can all be found in season. Some are imported, but they are augmented by cheaper local fruits such as dragon fruit. In Belize, the availability of local produce changes with the seasons so you need to appreciate each fruit in its own season, unlike the year-round availability we take for granted in more developed countries.

Chicken, pork and grains are produced mainly by the Mennonites, along with cheese and dairy products. However, the limited availability of vegetarian and soy products would make living as a vegetarian extremely difficult in Belize. Rice, and beans of all kinds, are staples of Belizean cuisine. Learning to adapt to new recipes can take advantage of what is readily available.

Chocolate is becoming more available in Belize, particularly at specialty stores where you can now find high cocoa content quality chocolate.

Some things I missed and was surprised at not being able to obtain in Belize included fresh tuna and salmon (although there are plenty more fresh fish species to choose from), peaches, mixed greens, arugula, spinach, berries, decaffeinated coffee, breakfast cereals and low-calorie items such as low-fat cream cheese and diet/low-calorie soft drinks.

Although you may be determined to "live like a local" and avoid imported specialty items, it is hard to do without some basics such as seasonings, spices, sauces, olive oil, balsamic vinegar and pine nuts. Some of these are available in Belize at a price, particularly in shops such as Wine de Vine on Ambergris Cay. Mostly you have to stock up when you return to the US or Europe on a family visit and then hoard your treasures!

Although lobster and snapper are available in Belize, so too are meats from iguanas and gibnuts, (small rat-like rodents) which I found hard to even consider eating. An open mind and a willingness to adapt without complaining are two essentials you must have to survive when living in Belize!

## 12. Shopping

Anyone who requires a regular top-up of retail therapy will find they need to leave Belize to do so. There are no big named brands or chain stores such as Sams Club, Target, Macy's, Michaels or Wal-Mart to pick up your favorite household items and clothing. However, you can get everything you need to live a simple life here; just little choice and no brand names.

For fashion, quality household items and to get your Rolex watch serviced, you may need to make regular trips to the USA.

Shopping in Belize ranges from dusty streets and a few poorly stocked shops in Belize City to the tourist-oriented shops in the lively town of San Pedro. Reggae music can be heard in the bars and street cafés on the cayes where there are more shops and restaurants catering for high-end tourists.

Although bartering is acceptable on markets, generally shop prices are fixed. In the quieter off-season you can politely enquire if there are discounts off hotels rooms, dive trips etc. and get a better deal.

Regular opening hours for shops and businesses is from 8am to 5pm. Many independent shops close for lunch from 1pm to 2pm but they are open on weekends.

One option open to those considering living in Corozal in northern Belize is the chance to hop over the Mexican border to Chetumal for a more American-style shopping experience. Wholesale food stores such as Sam's Club can be found here along with an Office Depot, Walmart and a Bodega Aurrera.

The Plaza Las Americas opened in 2002 and has well-stocked stores for clothing, household and beauty products as well as a food court and multi-screen cinema. Many films are actually in English with Spanish subtitles.

The downtown area has many more independent shops offering specialty items such as pet food, craft supplies, sports equipment, hardware and locksmiths' inventory. Plenty of choice and many bargains can also be found on the open-air markets in Chetumal which are known simply as the New Market and the Old Market.

## 13. Language

Photo: R Barraez D´Lucca

One of the big surprises about Belize is that English is spoken everywhere as it is still the official language. Although many locals speak Mestizo (Hispanic Belizean) or Kriol at home, they still communicate easily in English.

Although English is the primary language in Belize, you will still find it challenging to be understood. Belizeans do not communicate in the same way as North Americans or Europeans. Keep your words and language slow and simple and be specific when asking questions.

Belizeans tend to respond quickly without giving time for your question to register. If their answer simply does not make sense, it is probably because they are answering the question they thought you were going to ask.

Like many South Americans, they want to please and will often give you the answer they think you want to hear, although it may not necessarily be accurate. For example, if you ask them for directions to a place to eat and then ask them if the food is good they will invariably give a glowing report, even if they know the food is terrible. They simply want to give you a positive answer.

In another example, at a conference I attended the microphone stopped working. The speaker turned to the IT specialist and asked him if the microphone was working. He replied, "Yes, it's working" but then left the room to attend to the problem.

Like everything, the language in Belize and the culture associated with it may take some adapting to.

On the positive side, many TV stations are in English, as are books, magazines and newspapers, when you can find them.

## 14. Political Stability

One thing hugely in Belize's favor is that it is considered a politically and economically stable country. It is run as a Parliamentary Democracy with the government made up of three arms: legislative, executive and judicial.

Within the legislative branch there is a House of Representatives, with 29 publically elected members, and a Senate with 12 government-appointed Senators. The Queen remains the Head of State and she appoints the Governor General to represent her. The Governor General in turn appoints the Prime Minister from within the House of Representatives.

In the past, Belize has been rife with corruption including in the government and police force. More recently, the new government has more credibility internationally although those considering moving to Belize may still find pockets of corruption just as anywhere else in the world.

## 15. Local Behavior

People in Belize are generally smiling and friendly outside of places like the grim port area of Belize City where crime is generally higher. The main social problems in Belize tend to stem from lack of education, poverty and drugs.

There are many cultural differences and expats inevitably must be the ones to adapt, not vice versa. For some, this initial adjustment comes easily, but others may find the local attitude frustrating, particularly when something needs to be done as a matter of urgency.

Belizeans are naturally proud of their culture and are very independent. They do not tolerate criticism of their country, even though they know its inadequacies and shortfalls. It is important to be tolerant and polite in order to be accepted, and this may require a lot of tongue-biting when, by nature, you want to make suggestions for obvious improvements. Unfortunately it will only be considered as criticism.

Getting services, even government services such as a visa, can be frustrating slow, repetitive and tedious and you need to remain cool and polite when dealing with local officials. Anger and an impatient attitude generally get you nowhere, in fact it often results in an even slower rate of progress.

However, persistence in following your applications up daily in a courteous polite manner at least prevents your application from being totally ignored.

Reliability and customer service are often lacking in business, but so too are stress and impatience. You will often find small businesses may be closed for no apparent reason. Making your move to Belize a happy success will inevitably mean learning to live with Belize "as is".

## 16. Security

Most visitors to Belize feel relatively safe, but there is the usual element of petty crime against wealthy tourists. Burglaries of homes and condos are common, so security doors and bars on the windows are a sensible precaution. Cocaine and drugs are present, even on Ambergris Caye, and are often the underlying cause of local crime, theft, robbery and even murder.

As with any other country, take sensible precautions after dark. Leave valuable watches and jewelry at home to avoid becoming a target for crime. Locals naturally view expats as wealthy because they judge them by their lifestyle. Owning a car and eating in a restaurant for many working Belizeans is simply not possible. Inevitably this leads to some resentment which in the minority of cases may result in opportunistic theft.

The main area of hotels and businesses in Belize City is relatively safe by day, but after dark it is certainly not safe to be on the streets as a white tourist. There is a strong police presence but places such as Belize City are not the place to consider living as an ex-pat.

## 17. Climate

The tropical climate in Belize is one of the attractions that makes people consider moving here permanently. The climate is consistently hot for most of the time, especially in coastal areas. In winter, daytime temperatures are in the low 80s and in the upper 50s overnight. The rest of the year enjoys daytime temperatures in the 80s and low 90s with overnight lows in the 70s. Humidity is high.

It can be windy with chilly "Northers" blowing in winter. The wettest months are from July to November which creates more oppressive humidity. The rain also creates perfect breeding conditions for vicious biting insects such as mosquitos, sand flies and no-see-ums.

The hurricane season in Belize runs from June to November. To keep things in perspective, since 1930 the country has only had 16 hurricanes (defined by wind speeds exceeding 75 mph) and a further 17 tropical storms (wind speeds exceeding 39 mph) making landfall. However, any major tropical storm system in the Caribbean can cause high winds and rainfall during this season.

## 18. Insects

Belize is a tropical country and consequently does have more bugs and insects than you may be used to elsewhere. There are poisonous snakes, scorpions and spiders to be aware of. Mosquitoes are less of a problem in beach areas and where there are prevailing sea breezes. Most resorts spray to keep the mosquito population down.

Unlike Florida, there are no bug screens or enclosures on homes in Belize so if, like my wife, you suffer from bites from no-see-ums and mosquitos, evenings can be an ordeal. Even though she regularly applied insect repellant she still got some nasty bites and itchy red lumps on her body on a daily basis. Using insect repellant containing deet is not entirely successful, so it is advisable to cover up with light pants, socks and long sleeves to avoid being bitten. For anyone who has a reaction to insect bites, these insects can cause ongoing misery and an inability to sleep.

Mosquitos are more of a problem in undeveloped areas, and after rainy spells. As well as causing red itchy lumps when they bite, mosquitos are the carriers of diseases including malaria and dengue fever which are both extremely serious conditions that can kill.

More information on the effects of dengue fever, including how to avoid contracting it, can be found in the book "Surviving Dengue Fever" which is available on Amazon.com. While a first encounter with the disease has serious and long-lasting after-effects, a second dose is likely to penetrate the brain barrier or cause hemorrhagic fever, both of which have a high mortality rate. Doctors warn that anyone who has already had dengue fever should avoid visiting or living anywhere that dengue fever is endemic, such as Belize.

On beaches, sandflies can be a problem, especially at dusk. Use insect repellant whenever you take a trip into the jungle or visit freshwater lakes and rivers. Most insects bite in the evening so use a repellant or cover your skin if you plan to sit outdoors. Some bites and stings can be harmful and may cause serious health problems days or even weeks later.

Belize has no poison control center so in the case of being bitten by a snake, or having an encounter with a poisonous spider, plant or fish, it is best to get the patient to a hospital or local medical center as soon as possible. It is wise to acquaint yourself with your surroundings and brush up your basic knowledge so you can recognize a potentially poisonous snake or sea creature and know how to perform basic first aid. Professional help could be a long way off!

## 19. Standards of Dress

Casual dress is the order of the day in Belize. Most people live and do business wearing just a shirt or t-shirt and shorts. If you are really dressing up, a collared shirt and khakis for men and a casual dress for women is sufficient. If you're looking for a more formal lifestyle, Belize is not the place for you.

## 20. Hair and Beauty

A visit to the local beauty salon, if you can find one, is likely to be very different experience in Belize. There are local barbers and hairdressers but techniques such as highlighting, coloring your hair and other specialist hair treatments are rarely found. The best place to find these services is within a luxury hotel spa.

Manicures, pedicures and acrylic nail services are not commonly available and there is little demand for them. Massages, facials and other beauty treatments do not exist outside luxury hotels and if you do find them, prices are likely to be high.

## 21. Pets

Healthy pets can be imported into Belize without quarantine. You must travel with the required paperwork from a government approved vet, i.e. the APHIS 7001 International Health Certificate issued on behalf of the U.S. Department of Agriculture. It should show that your pet was examined within 14 days of the move and has been vaccinated for certain diseases.

Dogs must be vaccinated for parvo, distemper, infectious canine hepatitis, leptospirosis and rabies.

Cats must be vaccinated against feline calicivirus (FCV), viral rhinotracheitis (FVR) and panleucopaenia. The animal will be examined on arrival for any signs of ill health or wounds.

Further information can be obtained from the Belize Agricultural Health Authority (BAHA). There is a fee for importing any animal to Belize as well as considerable paperwork to be completed well ahead of the pet's arrival in the country.

There is no policy for picking up after your pet, which can be a mixed blessing when it comes to walking the streets or beaches, especially if you do not have a pet yourself. It's all part of living in Belize.

Finding branded pet food and suitably qualified vets can be a challenge.

You should also consider whether your pet will be able to adapt to the hot, humid climate of Belize, particularly if you are moving from a colder climate. It may be kinder to find them a new home if you have a dog with a thick fur coat that will simply be miserable and uncomfortable living in a climate they were never destined to endure.

Photo: Roger Wollstadt

## 22. Running a Car

There are two important rules for drivers in Belize: driving is on the right side of the road and wearing a seat belt is compulsory.

Most Belizeans do not own or run a vehicle. The more fortunate ones with a steady job in Belmopan or Belize City may own a motor scooter. For most locals, owning a vehicle is well beyond their wildest dreams.

Expats may choose to import a car from overseas. A four-wheel-drive truck is usually the best option for navigating the rough roads and tracks. More information about road surfaces is covered later in Chapter 24 on Environment, Sanitation and Infrastructure. In more established localities such as expat communities on Ambergris Caye, golf carts can be the most practical and economical way to get around.

Repairs and spare parts can be difficult to source for cars. It is best to choose a reliable runner and a common make such as Ford or Toyota to make it easier to find parts and a mechanic experienced with your particular make of vehicle.

Bringing a vehicle to Belize can be expensive, not only because of the shipping costs, but also because of the additional import duty.

Duty ranges from 20-70% of the vehicle's worth. Import duty is calculated on the value and size of engine of the car, or gross weight plus engine size for trucks. Unfortunately, you are at the mercy of the customs and excise officers to calculate the value of your vehicle for duty, plus adding appropriate sales tax and an environmental tax. For older vehicles it can work out more than the vehicle is actually worth.

However, under the Qualified Retired Persons Program (QRP) you may be entitled to bring in a vehicle duty-free every five years which is well worth taking advantage of. There are similar tax benefits for importing a boat or light aircraft.

You need to have all the original documents relating to the vehicle and are obliged to buy insurance in Belize immediately after the vehicle has cleared customs.

Gas/petrol prices are much higher than in the USA as vehicles are considered luxury items and are taxed accordingly.

Rental cars are available from the airport, but again they are far more expensive than the USA. Second hand cars tend to be scarce, expensive and in poor repair. Many will have been used as taxis and have exceptionally high mileage and a poor service history.

## 23. Local Transport

Buses are a cheap, safe and an easy way to get around while you are searching for a place to live. Intercity buses use the four paved highways (Northern, Western, Southern and Hummingbird highways). While some are plush air-conditioned coaches, other vehicles are repurposed former U.S. school buses with three people sharing each double seat.

Taxis can be found around the airport and in most major towns. Look for authorized licensed taxis which have green license plates.

Belize taxis do not have meters, so agree a price for your trip before you get in. There will be an additional price for more than one passenger. Tips are not customary but are always appreciated, especially if the driver has carried your bags or given you a commentary of the local sights along the way.

Water taxis are the usual transport between Belize City, San Pedro, Caye Caulker and other smaller cayes. Expect to pay at least BZ$20 for the 90-minute journey from Belize City to San Pedro.

Other water taxis connect San Pedro with Chetumal and Corozal. These boats are around 40 feet long, carry about 40 passengers and travel at speed over the sometimes choppy waters. Most boats are open to the elements so you and your bags may get covered in salt spray. Life jackets are not compulsory.

Mountain bikes are a good way to get around locally in the quieter districts. Motorcycles and scooters can be rented by the hour or by the day. However, the unpaved roads and poor standards of local driving can make this a hazardous option.

Ambergris Caye is totally different from any other part of Belize. The reason I mention it in the transport section is that the island is easy to get around by golf cart, which is the main form of transport on the island. Privately owned cars require a permit from the council and car rentals are not permitted on the island.

Golf carts are available to buy, or to hire for around US$40 a day; US$250 per week, basically about as expensive as a rental car anywhere else. You can choose from electric or gas-powered carts.

## 24. Environment, Sanitation and Infrastructure

Belizean infrastructure compared to developed countries is almost non-existent. It is gradually improving from dirt tracks to gravel and now has four main paved roads (Northern, Western, Southern and Hummingbird highways). Even short journeys between towns can take much longer than anticipated due to the winding, indirect routes and poor road surface conditions. With just 300,000 residents it is understandably hard for the government to find the funds to repair the existing infrastructure, let alone develop new roads. There is no railway system.

On Ambergris Caye you will find some of the main streets paved with concrete cobblestones while the side streets are still made of sand. Outside San Pedro the dirt roads are shared by all forms of transport, from golf carts and motor scooters to tour buses, bicycles and pedestrians.

Belize City has many rough streets with filthy open sewers running along the gutter. Metal grids are a nasty tripping hazard. I know of one friend who tripped while wearing leather sandals and cut open his toe. Unfortunately a nasty infection quickly set in and hospital treatment was required. Standards of infrastructure are much lower than most visitors are used to, so extra care is advised and plenty of antiseptic bathing is recommended in the event of even a simple cut or abrasion to avoid infection setting in.

## 25. Family Life and Education in Belize

Family life for youngsters in Belize is very different from other more developed countries. Video games, sports facilities and movie theaters are few and far between. Most children certainly do not own cell phones. Children moving to Belize need to learn a whole new set of rules to keep them safe. They need to know not to pat stray dogs as they may have rabies and to be aware of deadly snakes, insects and poisonous fruits or plants.

In Belize, women are responsible for keeping the house, cooking and child rearing. Men often have to leave their families behind when they go in search of work. Having multiple partners is common and single parent households are the norm rather than the exception.

When mothers find work they have no option but to leave their young children in the care of relatives or leave them home alone to fend for themselves. Older children often have to drop out of school and take care of younger siblings or find a job to help support the family financially.

Those moving to Belize with a young family should look carefully into the issue of education. Many expat families choose home schooling, but finding access to the curriculum and sourcing workbook material is difficult. Standards of education in Belize are improving, but less than 40% of school teachers have any formal training so standards vary widely.

For permanent residents, schooling is free and school buses collect children from rural areas and transport them to and from school.

Schooling for Belizean children is compulsory up to the age of 14 but is rarely enforced. The dropout rate at a younger age is considerable. The literacy rate in Belize is 77%. One issue that may be of concern to immigrants is that corporal punishment is still part of life in Belize in homes, schools and police detention centers.

Private schools are few and far between and expensive. They are generally located in Belize City and on Ambergris Cay.

Belize has two universities; Galen University and the University of Belize (UB) which has several campuses. Public schools are funded jointly by the government and the Roman Catholic Church. As a result, Catholic holidays are observed, religious instruction is taught and uniforms are worn. Classes are taught in English.

Secondary schools are often known as colleges and an entrance exam is required to determine which school your child can attend. There is a fee for non-nationals, generally of around $300 per year on top of uniform, text books and supplies which can add several hundred dollars per year. At the end of Grade 11, students can sit the Caribbean Examinations Council exams and the certificates are recognized internationally.

## 26. Social Life

Belizeans love to party and their festivities can often last all night with loud music and dancing. Music is played unbelievably loudly from huge speakers making the very ground shake around the amplifiers at festivals and street events. Even *quinceanera* celebrations, when a young girl celebrates her 15<sup>th</sup> birthday, can go on until the next morning.

Churches are lively social centers with music booming from the amplifiers and everyone singing and dancing, not necessarily in tune. You can't help but smile and appreciate that what is lacking in expertise is more than made up for in enthusiasm.

Like much of South America, festivals in Belize are plentiful and are very much part of the local culture. If deafening music is not your thing, you either need to live somewhere remote or escape when local festivals such as Santa Semana (Easter) and other events are celebrated. While some ex-pats are happy to join in and "go with the flow", others find it wearing to have their sleep disturbed.

## 27. Hobbies and Social Activities

You will certainly not find the usual sports opportunities or social craft and hobby groups in Belize but in San Ignacio, Ambergris Caye and elsewhere there are opportunities for volunteering and making a difference. Local Rotary Clubs are active and have many ongoing projects to make a real difference in needy communities. Many expats become involved in local projects to benefit the communities in which they have chosen to reside. Those willing to contribute to the wellbeing of others will find plenty of opportunities for philanthropic projects in Belize which can be a means of finding like-minded expats and joining in the social life that inevitably exists around such endeavors.

One project which the Rotary Club funded typically illustrates the problems which are exacerbated by the poor standards of education. In many areas the lack of safe drinking water as a basic requirement is of great concern. It causes unnecessary sickness, poor school attendance and a host of easily preventable health related issues. Even those with a piped supply of drinking water are at risk as the cisterns are contaminated with e-coli and other bacteria which cause infections.

As a trial, the Rotarians provided ten water filtration systems (two buckets and a kidney dialysis filter to strain out the smallest impurities) to families in San Mateo on Ambergris Caye. They were trained in how to use the simple water filters and were taught the benefits of doing so. In following up on the 10 sample families after a few months, it became very clear that things that westerners take for granted are a challenge for local Belizeans.

The families using the water filters reported that their family health had improved and were grateful for the equipment. One family had given their filter away to someone who they felt had greater need than they did of the clean water and one of the elderly women admitted she did not know what the system was for. Her husband had attended the training course but never taught his wife how to use it so the equipment was in its original state, totally unused. Once the woman was taught how to use the filter she was delighted and wished she had known how to use it earlier.

Misunderstanding arose in some cases as some families only used the filter system to treat the rainwater caught in their cisterns. They felt the tap water was too dirty for the filters to have any effect, which was certainly not the case. Another family used the filtered water for their older children but bought bottled water for their baby as they simply didn't trust the water filter system.

Unfortunately some families used the buckets for garbage and other uses which negated the benefits of them using the buckets for filtering the water. Providing locals with new devices to improve their standard of living needs to be accompanied by careful training to dispel myths and overcome distrust.

## 28. Sporting Activities in Belize

Although Belize has an extensive Caribbean coastline, it has few sandy beaches. Most of the shoreline is lined with mangrove swamps. This can come as a nasty surprise for many visitors who envisage beautiful white sandy beaches. The best place to find typical Caribbean beaches is on the southern coast of Belize or on the offshore cayes such as Ambergris Caye, as outlined in the first chapter.

Surfers will be sadly disappointed too. Belize has almost no wave action and certainly has no lifeguards. Long Caye at Glover's Reef is an exception and offers a surf break which is mercifully free from the sharp corals that can be perilous elsewhere.

For me, one of the most off-putting problems about Belize beaches is the amount of garbage that litters the tidemark. Most of it has been tossed overboard by thoughtless boaters and unfortunately Belize has no official beach clean-up patrols. Adding to the problem are all the cans, trash and even diapers left by other beach users and the result can be vile.

If you are looking for an all-over suntan, Belize is certainly not the place for you. Nudity is illegal and you certainly do not want to find yourself subjected to the Belizean criminal justice system.

Ambergris Caye is the best place for those looking for watersports activities and things to do. Sailing, diving in the Blue Hole, snorkeling on the fabulous Belize Reef, fishing, parasailing and kiteboarding are all available here.

The amount of coastal sea grass generally means that snorkeling opportunities are limited from the beach. You generally need to take a short boat ride to reach the reef itself.

**Golf in Belize**

Belize has not had a golf course since British colonial days, so the newly built golf course on the small private island of Caye Chapel is actually making history. The 18-hole golf course on Caye Chapel is located south of Cape Caulker, a 45-minute boat trip from San Pedro.

Built as part of the Caye Chapel Island Resort and Marina, the par-72 course is very beautiful, but even by golfing standards it is not cheap. Day packages including a golf cart and use of the swimming pool and private beach are around US$200 per day.

The course was designed mostly by the island's American owner, Larry Addington. It required the import of a special hybrid grass called *Paspalum* which requires less fertilizer, pesticides and water than traditional fairway greens to reduce the danger of run-off harming the surrounding reefs and marine life.

Although Belize has an ideal golfing climate, those looking for a cheap Florida-style place to retire and play golf will find Belize is totally inadequate when it comes to sports such as golf, tennis, bowling and bocce.

## Diving and Watersports

One thing that Belize does better than almost anywhere else in the world is diving. With the pristine Belize Reef lying just offshore, and easy access to the great Blue Hole, snorkelers and scuba divers can forgive some of Belize's shortcomings in exchange for having this stunning water playground right on their doorstep.

The Blue Hole appears darkly in the midst of the otherwise clear aquamarine waters and it predates the Ice Age. This 400-foot-deep limestone sinkhole has to be one of the world's most thrilling natural wonders with myriad angelfish, elkhorn corals, stalactites and cleaner shrimp. The Blue Hole is one of seven separate sites on the Belize Barrier Reef Reserve System that are listed as UNESCO World Heritage Sites.

The Caribbean waters surrounding the cayes provide some of the best snorkeling and diving in the world with corals, turtles and schools of brightly colored fish to watch and marvel at. Larger fish such as barracudas, rays and reef sharks can also be seen.

Belize is home to endangered manatees which breed and feed in the warm waters of Belize's lagoons, rivers and estuaries. Unfortunately, their slow swimming, poor eyesight and docile attitude mean they are frequent victims of accidents with boat propellers.

All these natural underwater attractions remain as yet unexploited, but despite their proximity to mainland Belize, diving and snorkeling trips remain quite expensive. However, dives do tend to be in smaller groups accompanied by suitably qualified PADI dive masters.

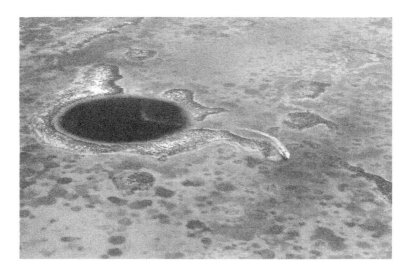

Photo: Jetske

## 29. Eating Out and Nightlife

There is an enormous range of opportunities for eating out in Belize, depending upon where you are living or staying. Street vendors sell tacos for under US$1, if you fancy your chances with the lack of refrigeration and lax hygiene. Burger bars and pizzerias offer fast food which in places like San Pedro will be similar in price to Florida.

Ambergris Caye has the best social life for expats with organized events and several good restaurants. Friday evening is the night for cheese and wine at the local Wine de Vine. The best place to find upscale dining is in a luxury resort or hotel. Best value dining in Belize is a fresh seafood or lobster dinner in a top restaurant which will cost around $30.

Outside the hotel resorts and cities, nightlife is limited. Another problem is that Belize City and Belmopan are considered unsafe for expats and foreigners to be out on the streets at night. They are an easy target for robbery, mugging and worse.

The Belize Free Zone is an interesting area, located about seven miles south of the Mexican border in Corozal. Designed as a Commercial Free Zone (CFZ) to attract foreign business investment, it gives business entrepreneurs, wholesalers, importers and exporters some unique tax-free benefits on merchandise that is for direct export. The CFZ has a couple of nice hotels and casinos that provide floor shows and gambling for those wanting to sample more typical nightlife.

## 30. Tipping

Tipping in Belize is similar to the USA, although do check that the service charge is not already included in your bill. A 10-15% tip is the norm for good service, although you will generally only find this in hotel restaurants where some kind of training has been given on what "service" actually entails.

On the other hand, you may want to tip simply to give waiting staff the chance to support their families. Sometimes tipping in developing countries such as Belize is more about philanthropy and encouraging an enthusiastic work ethic, rather than for the level of service actually received.

Tipping is generally expected in restaurants, bars, for tour guides and for hotel services such as maids and bellhops. It is also usual to tip diving instructors about US$5 per tank.

Taxi drivers do not expect a tip, although if they have assisted with your luggage or shopping, a small tip is always appreciated.

## 31. Drinking Alcohol

The legal drinking age in Belize is 18, but it is rarely enforced. The most common drinks in Belize are the local Belikin Beer, or Fanta as a non-alcoholic alternative. Belikin has a distinctive picture of the Altun Ha Maya Temple on the label. This light beer costs around $2-3 in a tourist bar and slightly less in a local bar or from a supermarket. American beers are offered in tourist destinations but are even more expensive.

Prices remain higher than in neighboring Mexico as Bowen and Bowen has a virtual monopoly on the drinks trade in Belize. Other drinks they produce include Belikin Stout, Lighthouse Lager and Guinness Stout under license.

Cheap spirits include Belizean Rum (white or gold) costing $2-3 in bars and US$9 upwards for a bottle in a supermarket.

Branded sodas such as Coca-Cola are widely available but there are few sugar-free "diet" options. There are no supermarket own brands.

## 32. Drugs

Cocaine, marijuana and other drugs are widely available in Belize despite there being strict laws governing the sale and use of these illegal drugs. Visitors may be approached by locals offering drugs for sale, but it is not worth taking the risk.

The penalty for being found in possession of even a small quantity of illegal drugs is a fine and immediate deportation or imprisonment.

While some locals may not be deterred by a spell in prison, and openly smoke marijuana in public, for expats, a third-world prison sentence is likely to be a horrendous and dangerous experience.

## 33. Belizean Social Culture

Naturally you should expect there to be some differences when moving to a new country, continent and culture. Belizeans tend to avoid physical contact so greeting someone with a hug or a kiss would be deemed inappropriate between locals. Even shaking hands tends to be a light touch rather than a hearty grip. If you intend to conduct business in Belize, these are definitely things to be aware of to avoid offending local clients and officials.

Belizeans tend to avoid eye contact and remain deferential. One thing you will learn is that above all they want to please you. They will often give you the answer they think you want to hear, rather than the truth. They will also give you an answer even if they do not understand the question, which can be frustrating at times.

Other practicalities are common sense; do not openly criticize the country and its people and avoid the topics of politics and religion which most Belizeans consider taboo in business circles.

Women are generally respected. Although they are the traditional homemakers and child-raisers, they are increasingly holding more important roles in government and business.

## 34. Cultural and Religious Challenges

Although a slower pace of life may be exactly what you are looking for in your new home, you need to consider whether you can realistically adapt to a *manyana* attitude when it comes to services or urgent needs.

Belizeans typically do not have any perception of time, especially for specific appointments. Even public transport services do not adhere to the published timetable.

If you are serious about moving to Belize and making a new life there, the best way to cope with the different culture is to adapt. You will certainly not be able to change the country's standards; better to relax and adapt into its laid-back ways to avoid creating the stress you are probably moving to Belize to escape from.

Most local churches are Catholic. Masses are offered in English and in Spanish in some churches. There are also a variety of protestant and mission churches represented.

There are just two mosques: one in Belize City and another in Belmopan. Jews living in Belize City do not currently have a temple but meet in local homes.

## 35. Banking in Belize

Belize is a banking haven which was created by the British in 1981 and modeled upon the most successful offshore banking systems at that time. Although banking law has changed dramatically since 9/11, Belize's banking law remains quietly off-radar. The country continues to have banking, tax and financial advantages that few people are aware of.

Belize banks are impressively secure and stable with a required minimum liquidity ratio of 24%, compared to many other developed countries with a liquidity ratio of less than 10%. Despite tighter banking laws elsewhere in the world, particularly for American citizens, most visitors can open an account at Caye Bank with as little as US$1,000. Banks usually require a reference from your home bank on headed stationery and signed by a manager. It should state your reliability as a customer and the current balance in your account.

Banking is relatively easy in Belize. There are bank branches in all major towns and cities including Belize Bank, Alliance Bank, First Caribbean International and Atlantic Bank. There is also Caye Bank on Ambergris Caye, which is an international offshore bank.

ATM machines at Belize Bank and Atlantic Bank generally accept overseas ATM cards and there is a user fee of around $2 charged by the branch, as well possible further fees charged by your own bank. ATMs pay out Belize dollars.

## 36. Visas for Belize

Every visitor to Belize must have a passport which is valid for at least six months beyond the planned departure date. One positive advantage of visiting Belize is that visas are not currently required for visitors from the USA, Canada, UK, European Union, Australia and New Zealand to stay up to one month, so initial stays of up to 30 days are no problem. Thereafter, stays can be extended through the Belize Immigration Office for a fee. However, this could change so you should check the latest information.

There is a departure tax from Belize which is currently US$35, payable at Belize International Airport. Those departing by land will pay a local departure tax at the point of exit.

There are plans to improve Belize's retiree program, including making it easier for retirees to obtain Belizean citizenship after living in the country for five years.

Currently, in 2014, there are three options for staying in the country long-term:

1.    On arrival you will receive a 30-day visitor permit which can be renewed on a monthly basis at your local Department of Immigration Office, for up to one year. This is a good option for your first year if you are considering moving to Belize or planning a fact-finding visit to check out the possibilities without making any final decisions. The cost of renewal is BZ$50 (US$25) per month for the first 6 months and BZ$100 (US$50) per month thereafter.

You can rent a house during this period but you cannot work, even if the work is unpaid or voluntary. If you want to work you will need to acquire a work permit.

2.   After one year in the country, you can apply for official permanent residency. This negates the need for a work permit if you have a job and it allows you to run a business. Once you have been granted permanent residency, you can also travel in and out of the country without any restrictions. After five years you can apply for citizenship.

Although in theory the application sounds straightforward, most expats tell me it is frustrating, time consuming and expensive. Expect to make several visitors to Belmopan Department of Immigration in person to chase the progress of your application, and you will be called several times for appointments and interviews.

It can take up to a year to obtain and during that time you can only leave the country for 14 consecutive days. In the meantime you need to continue to apply for monthly extensions to your visitor permit and pay the obligatory BZ$100 each time.

One note of caution -- it is best not to mail any application or document as it simply will not arrive where it should. Instead, deliver everything in person even if it involves a special trip to Belmopan. In the long run, personal delivery is faster than losing your paperwork in the mail system, chasing it, obtaining replacements and then taking it in person.

3.    If you are over 45 and have a provable income or pension of at least US$24,000 per year, you can apply for the Qualified Retired Person (QRP) Program. This was developed to encourage retirees with income to move to Belize. To maintain this status you need to live in Belize for a minimum of one month per year.

The basic cost of acquiring the QRP visa is just over US$2000 per person. Legal and professional fees need to be added on top of this.

One advantage of the QRP is that you have a one-off opportunity in the first year to import personal effects including a vehicle into the country tax and duty free. The nominal worth must not exceed US$15,000.

I heard several accounts of the valuation of vehicles being set by Belizean officials as far higher than their true worth in order to charge duty when the total imports exceeded the tax-free limit, so it may be easier to simply buy a car in Belize.

## 37. Working in Belize

Most jobs are either in the agricultural or tourism industries. Belizeans naturally protect jobs for locals, especially as unemployment is currently over 11%.

Finding work can be challenging for ex-pats unless you are technically trained in skills that are in particularly short supply. However, Belize can be a good place for those who work from home or have their own internet business.

Local wages are unlikely to support a westernized lifestyle. The minimum wage is BZ$3.00 to $3.30, depending upon the industry, and the average annual wage is BZ$8,500. Working conditions are also not up to those of more developed nations, so human rights and labor laws are often disregarded.

Be aware that with a Qualified Retired Person's Visa you are not legally allowed to work in Belize. Residents must have either a Temporary Employment Permit or a Self-Employed Permit to allow them to work.

## 38. Starting a Business in Belize

Although I did not get as far as starting a company in Belize, I did meet two separate businessmen (one American, the other British) who were specifically looking to start a business. One was interested in operating a call center from Belize; the other was looking to run a sales center. Both decided in the end that Belize was not the place for them.

Belize offers corporations, LLCs, trusts and foundations as a vehicle for commercial or asset protection. Currently you need a local corporation if you actually plan to do business; otherwise an International Business Corporation (IBC) will suffice.

Those requiring a holding structure for investments or a trust should take legal advice as laws change regularly and it is important to understand the full implications before making such important decisions.

It is not easy to set up and run a business in Belize and getting reliable staff is even more difficult. Due to the low purchasing power and lack of disposable income you are unlikely to make your fortune with a Belize-based company. However, if you are running an internet company to worldwide customers and are not dependent upon local staff or efficient international delivery then you may be in with a chance.

Sadly Belize seems to be its own worst enemy with a poor work ethic and lack of drive, even in those who are offered a well-paid job.

The infrastructure is not set up to encourage business and the pace of life and attitudes in general are more laid back than some other Central and South American countries such as Nicaragua, Panama, Chile and Ecuador.

One exception to this is the Mennonite community which has a huge positive impact on Belize. Now well-established in Belize, it is the Mennonites that raise livestock and provide meat for the country. They also make good use of their traditional trades as carpenters and produce beautiful hand-made furniture and wooden homes.

## 39. Taxes

There is no capital gains tax in Belize but there are a number of other taxes that you may be liable for as a resident or homeowner in Belize.

Property Taxes are charged at 12.5% of the assessed rental value of your property if it is occupied and in an urban area, and 2% of the assessed rental value if unoccupied.

Land tax is charged to property owners at a flat rate of 1% of its value on all unimproved land.

Currently nonresidents are not taxed on their worldwide earnings but they are taxed on any Belize-sourced income.

If you receive rental income, business taxes are due on the gross rental income received, at a rate of 3%. This is payable monthly.

Income tax is payable on earnings but some expenses can be deducted first, including property taxes, repairs, mortgage payments and insurance.

## 40. Knowing the Law in Belize

Homosexuality is illegal and is technically an imprisonable offense. However there is a small but discreet gay scene in some of the main tourist centers and laws are rarely enforced. Caution and discretion should definitely be exercised in this area and even discussions on the topic are inadvisable.

Prostitution is also against the law but police tend to turn a blind eye unless the activity is blatant or officially reported by another person.

Drugs are also illegal and the government takes a very hard line against anyone found buying, selling or even in possession of drugs, however small a quantity. If you are offered drugs on the street or in a club, you are advised to decline and move on. It could be a trap and even if it isn't, it is definitely a criminal offence.

Owning an unlicensed firearm is illegal. Fines are high and repeat offenders will be given a jail sentence. If you plan to import a firearm you should contact the Belizean Embassy for advice.

One final matter to be aware of is that photographing official buildings is illegal and can be regarded as subversive activity. You should also check before taking photographs inside churches.

Purchasing or owning a pre-Columbian artifact is also illegal unless you have an official permit.

Prison life in Belize is certainly no holiday camp. Prisons are dirty, overcrowded and unsafe. Conditions certainly do not meet international standards and the death penalty is also still in place.

I heard several accounts of expats who found themselves in Belize Central Prison after a domestic dispute or other misunderstanding. They were dependent upon other expat friends to provide them with food, and getting legal representation was not easy.

If you are arrested, you need to insist upon your embassy being informed of your arrest otherwise it will not automatically be done and your stay may be unnecessarily extended. Belize has an extradition treaty in place with the USA, Cuba, Mexico and other member states of the British Commonwealth

## 41. Emergency Services

The emergency telephone number in Belize for calling all the emergency services (fire, police and ambulance) is 911 or 90. However, all the emergency services lack funding, equipment, training and manpower. They are run mainly by volunteers, particularly in the ambulance and fire services.

Even in urban areas, emergency services are very basic and unreliable and in rural areas they are non-existent. Response times are totally unpredictable so most people call on help locally with neighbors and strangers willingly lending a hand and offering assistance. However, this does not equate to life-saving equipment and experience in a life-or-death situation, a road accident or an accident in the home. It is often better to get to the nearest medical facility locally for medical attention rather than relying on the emergency services.

In its favor, if/when the emergency services do reach you they all speak English well enough to communicate with foreign visitors and expats.

The emergency infrastructure for those living in Belize is improving with help from other countries and support from nonprofit organizations. Vehicles are slowly being upgraded and medical staff are becoming more efficient.

### Ambulance

In Belize City, Belmopan and other larger towns there is a private ambulance service operated by the Belize Emergency Response Team (BERT). This non-profit organization has both ground and air ambulance services. Wings of Hope is another non-profit organization which operates an emergency air ambulance service.

All air ambulances are currently operated by volunteers and consist of a small plane or helicopter with a stretcher, oxygen and usually a trained paramedic volunteer. The downside for those with serious injuries is that patients are expected to make their own way to the airport for air transport to a hospital. Air ambulances scramble within 15 minutes of receiving a call. There is only room for one other person to accompany the injured person to hospital. As both these air ambulance services operate as a charity, patients are asked to make a donation. In some cases a nominal charge may be levied against those using the air ambulance services if the patient is deemed financially able to make a payment.

Regional hospitals can handle most emergency and lifesaving care but more serious conditions are transferred to Guatemala or Mexico once the patient is stable. If you live near the border with these countries it can be best to go straight over the border and receive the better care immediately.

Anyone planning to move to Belize needs to take heed and possibly attend a first aid training course before leaving their home country. It is important to know the basics in terms of dealing with a heart attack, fracture or stemming bleeding before professional help arrives. In the end, it could save a life; either of your spouse, family or someone else.

## Police

There is no doubt that the 1000-strong police force that is responsible for the whole country of Belize is woefully inadequate, which allows petty crime to go unchecked. Lack of funds, poor resources and a certain amount of corruption hamper the police efforts to be able to respond quickly and deal with reported criminal activity.

During periods of staff shortage or in times of emergency, the police force is bolstered by the Belize Defence Force

Crime rates overall are the same as in most other Central and South American countries with two exceptions: Belize City, which is far higher, and Ambergris Caye, which is much lower than the average. Violent crimes and crimes against tourists are taken more seriously by the police, who are keen to protect their fragile tourism business. Dedicated Tourism Police Officers can be found in major cities and can be identified by their navy pants, khaki shirts and navy hats.

## Fire

Although the ambulance and police services are stretched, by far the most inadequate emergency service in Belize is the fire service. Firefighters are undertrained and ill-equipped as most firefighting depends upon volunteers for manpower. However, those who continue to serve should be commended for doing their best with the few resources and little training they have.

Fire fighters aim to respond within 15 minutes of a 911 call, but it can often take 40 minutes for a crew to arrive. In rural areas the fire service is not available at all. The poor shanty-town buildings in Belize City are very susceptible to fire, which is a tragedy in an already terrible living situation.

Major cities and towns have from one to ten fire engines, generally donated cast-offs from other countries. Most are just basic pick-up trucks with a small water pump. Lack of fire hydrants add to the problems faced by the fire service so fire engines generally have to pump water from a local source such as a river, canal or lagoon.

## 42. Vaccinations

Visitors and those intending to move to Belize should be up-to-date on their routine vaccinations including:

- Measles-mumps-rubella (MMR)
- Diphtheria-tetanus-pertussis
- Chickenpox
- Polio

In addition government websites advise the following vaccines due to the increased risk in Belize:

- Hepatitis A (can be caught from contaminated water or food)
- Typhoid (can be caught from contaminated water and food, especially if eating local food or visiting rural areas)
- Rabies – particularly if you are moving to Belize long-term, will have contact with animals or plan to participate in outdoor activities such as hiking, camping and adventure travel.
- Hepatitis B if you are planning any sort of medical procedure, getting a tattoo or piercing, or having sex with a new partner
- Malaria is most common in the coastal lowlands. Talk to your doctor about taking precautions against malaria
- Dengue fever – there is currently no vaccination so you should take sensible precautions to avoid any mosquito bites

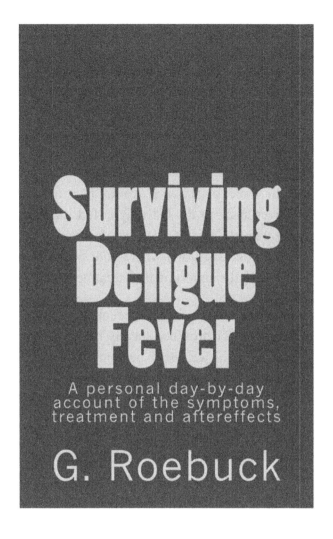

Belize does not have a risk of yellow fever. However, a yellow fever vaccination is compulsory for those entering Belize from a country that has a risk of yellow fever such as sub-Saharan African countries and parts of tropical South America. Documentary proof of having the vaccination is required.

## 43. Medical Services

Belize is a small country struggling to develop. Like many of its resources, its healthcare is limited and primitive. Should you fall sick, you will find dedicated general physicians who are familiar in dealing with local diseases but few highly qualified specialists and modern facilities.

You need to have plans in place to be transported to Mexico or even back to the U.S if you fall ill. Where you choose to be treated depends upon whether you are covered for Medicare in the USA, and where your health insurance, if any, covers you for major medical treatment.

Belize does not have a reciprocal agreement with the UK so all treatment, whether provided locally or in a neighboring country, must be paid for either personally or by claiming from a travel insurance or health insurance policy.

If you do need to be evacuated to obtain specialist emergency care, it can be expensive. Check the small print of any healthcare policy you have to see exactly what cover is covered beyond Belize. Repatriation may be an option, but all insurance needs to be in place before any medical condition is diagnosed, otherwise it is obviously excluded from cover on the basis of it being a pre-existing condition.

## 44. Healthcare

Standards of healthcare are typical of those in the Caribbean, and unfortunately well below those of some Central American countries such as Panama and Costa Rica. Every city and major town in Belize has a hospital or clinic although the lack of funds means that standards of care do not meet those found in North America or Europe.

The best facilities are in Belize City for those willing to pay privately or have suitable medical insurance cover. The main hospital is the Karl Heusner Memorial Hospital where those with serious medical conditions may be referred to for treatment. It does have some modern equipment such as a CAT-scanner but most patients are referred to private facilities where they must pay for lab tests or x-rays and the equipment is often nonfunctional.

There is no radiation therapy available at all in Belize and not a single doctor is qualified in oncology.

Belize has three regional hospitals: Southern Regional Hospital in Dangriga; Northern Regional Hospital in Orange Walk Town and the Western Regional Hospital in Belmopan. However the total number of public beds across all the hospitals is just 700, with a further 100 beds in the three private hospitals: La Loma Luz Hospital in San Ignacio; Belize Medical Associates, and Universal Health Services, both in Belize City.

There is a small hospital on Ambergris Caye and a clinic at Corozal Town Hospital but most expats are advised to seek better medical care over the border at Chetumal in Mexico or Melchor-Flores in Guatemala even for routine procedures such as hip and knee replacement surgery. The lack of healthcare is a sobering thought to bear in mind for anyone planning to retire to Belize.

Dental care is far more positive, with American trained dental surgeons providing high quality dental care privately at a considerably lower cost than in North America. A filling may cost around US$40 and a crown closer to US$350 in Belize.

## Conclusion

As you will have discovered, living in Belize is very different from living in a more developed country. If you are looking for somewhere totally different and are able to quit the rat race with all that that entails, then you may well be able to move to Belize and live happily ever after.

One important factor to note is that "developing" does not necessarily mean "cheap". Many magazines and companies specializing in retirement advice paint a rosy picture of an idyllic retirement in an exotic destination. Claims that you can live like a king on a state pension need to be taken with a pinch of salt and carefully analyzed.

I have read many glowing reports that describe eating out for next to nothing and having local staff to provide housekeeping and nursing care as you age. All these claims need to be realistically checked out for yourself through books, internet sources, talking to people who have made the move, and finally by visiting the country in person. Be particularly wary of reports made by someone with a vested interest in your move, such as a realtor or immigration-related business.

Questions you need to ask include:
Are you prepared to live in local housing with substandard services?
Can you envisage living in a country where utilities are sporadic and emergency services are limited?
Are your prepared to live thousands of miles from family and friends?

What healthcare do you think you may need as you age, and will you have access to medications, should your health deteriorate?

Most importantly, how far will your income actually stretch in your new country and can you really afford the necessities of life that you have come to expect?

Already there is a sizeable expat community in Belize for those who want to socialize with others from a similar background. However, the inconveniences and lack of amenities should not be ignored. A dramatic change in attitude, standard of living and expectations will be demanded from anyone planning to move to Belize. Despite the advantages of a tropical climate and attractive tax breaks, when I looked more closely at what Belize had to offer, I concluded that Moving to Belize was Not for Me.

I moved on from Belize to look at another Central American country for my retirement – the Republic of Panama. If you are interested in comparing life in Belize with life in Panama, you may also find my book *Moving to Panama – Not for Me* offers useful insight into that country's lifestyle too. While Panama is more developed than Belize, the more Latino lifestyle, language and culture present their own challenges.

I sincerely hope you find the paradise you are searching for that fulfills most, if not all, of your personal requirements and allows you to live the lifestyle you desire. Happy hunting!

## Useful Contacts

Belize Embassy in the USA
2535 Massachusetts Ave, NW, Washington D.C.
www.embassyofbelize.org

US Embassy in Belize
http://belize.usembassy.gov/

Canadian Embassy in Belize
http://www.canadianembassyinformation.com/embassy-in/belize.html

British Embassy in Belize
http://www.british-embassy.net/belize.html

U.S. Department of State Travel Advice on Belize
http://www.state.gov/r/pa/ei/bgn/1955.htm

# OTHER TITLES

Look out for more books by G. Roebuck:

## Moving to Panama – Not for Me!

While International Living continues to uphold Panama as one of the best places to retire, it is certainly not for everyone. This book covers over 40 different topics about living in Panama in eyewitness detail, from the unexpectedly high cost of electricity to alarming personal safety issues.

Read this book as if you are overhearing a conversation between two friends. Listen to the parallel story of a stranger taking a path that you might be considering, and read the true stories of other expats. Before you finally decided that Panama is the perfect retirement haven, you owe it to yourself to find out the negative side as well.

## Surviving Dengue Fever

Dengue fever is a deadly disease that can affect travelers of all ages visiting the tropics and subtropics. It is vital to take every precaution against mosquito bites to avoid contracting this disease. Arm yourself with knowledge about how the disease is spread and how to avoid it.

Having personally suffered dengue fever first hand, the author offers a day-by-day account of the symptoms and best ways to treat them. Hopefully you will never have to know these details, but to be forewarned is to be forearmed.

Made in the USA
Middletown, DE
13 January 2020